Minnesota

by Rebecca Stromstad Glaser

Consultant:
William E. Lass
History Professor Emeritus
Minnesota State
University, Mankato

Capstone Press
Mankato, Minnesota

Capstone Press
151 Good Counsel Drive • P.O. Box 669 • Mankato, Minnesota 56002
http://www.capstone-press.com

Printed in the United States of America

Library of Congress Cataloging-in-Publication Data
Glaser, Rebecca Stromstad.
Minnesota / by Rebecca Stromstad Glaser.
p. cm.—(Land of liberty)
Includes bibliographical references and index.
Contents: About Minnesota—Land, climate, and wildlife—History of Minnesota—Government and politics—Economy and resources—People and culture
ISBN 0-7368-1591-0 (hardcover)
1. Minnesota—Juvenile literature. [1. Minnesota.] I. Title. II. Series.
F606.3.G57 2003
977.6—dc21 2002011078

Summary: An introduction to the geography, history, government, politics, economy, resources, people, and culture of Minnesota, including maps, charts, and a recipe.

Editorial Credits

June Preszler, editor; Jennifer Schonborn, series designer; Linda Clavel, book designer; Angi Gahler, illustrator; Kelly Garvin, photo researcher; Eric Kudalis, product planning editor

Photo Credits

Cover images: Split Rock Lighthouse, James P. Rowan; New Verndale, Richard Hamilton Smith

Capstone Press/Amanda Doering, 4; Capstone Press/Gary Sundermeyer, 54; Corbis, 37; Corbis/ Annie Griffiths, 42; Corbis/Minnesota Historical Society, 24, 26, 30; Corbis/ Owaki-Kulla, 46; Corbis/Reuters NewMedia Inc., 50; Corbis/Wally McNamee, 39; Getty Images, 52–53; Hulton/Archive by Getty Images, 22; Kay Shaw, 8, 14–15, 32, 63; Minnesota Historical Society, 19; North Wind Picture Archives, 20–21, 29, 58; One Mile Up, Inc., 55 (both); PhotoDisc, Inc., 44–45; Richard Hamilton Smith, 12, 40; Robert McCaw, 56, 57; Stock Montage, Inc./The Newberry Library, 16; U.S. Postal Service, 59

Artistic Effects

Corbis, Creatas, Digital Stock, Digital Vision, PhotoDisc

1 2 3 4 5 6 08 07 06 05 04 03

Table of Contents

Every year, visitors to the Minnesota State Fair stroll through the fairgrounds on their way to exhibits, shows, rides, and contests.

Chapter 1

About Minnesota

Late August means State Fair to Minnesotans, both young and old. More than 1.7 million people gather at the state fairgrounds in St. Paul. The fair draws visitors from within the state and across the country.

Fairgoers compete in talent shows, view exhibits, and watch contests. People try to best one another in livestock shows, school projects, horsemanship, and baked goods. Visitors wander through Machinery Hill as they check out new tractors. Later, they may scream their way through an old-fashioned roller coaster ride.

By their visits' end, most fairgoers have tried at least one of nearly 30 foods on a stick. Chocolate lovers have smacked their lips for deep-fried Snickers bars on a stick. The more recent addition of deep-fried macaroni and cheese on a stick also draws crowds.

The fair is only one point of interest in this upper-Midwest state. Minnesota's land provides thick forests, huge prairies, flowing rivers, and sparkling lakes.

Sky-tinted Waters

Minnesota's name comes from a Dakota Indian word meaning "sky-tinted waters." The name fits. The state's more than 15,000 lake areas offer hiking, swimming, fishing, and boating.

Waters form many state borders. Canada lies above Lake Superior and the Boundary Waters. The Red River of the North and Bois de Sioux River separate Minnesota from North Dakota. The St. Croix and Mississippi Rivers form most of the eastern border. South Dakota is to the west. Iowa lies to the south.

Minnesota's population ranks 21st among the states. The 2000 Census counted 4,919,479 people in the state.

Minnesota Cities

The scenic Boundary Waters Wilderness Canoe Area includes five major lakes and 25 smaller ones.

Chapter 2

Land, Climate, and Wildlife

Minnesota is often called "The Star of the North." It has the most northern point in the lower 48 U.S. states. The Lake of the Woods area reaches into Canada.

Four geographical regions make up Minnesota's landscape. They are the Superior Upland, the Young Drift Plains, the Dissected Till Plains, and the Driftless Area.

Superior Upland

The rocky Superior Upland lies near Lake Superior in northeastern Minnesota. The lake's coast is only 602 feet (183 meters) above sea level. Minnesota's highest point, Eagle Mountain, is 2,301 feet (701 meters) above sea level.

The Superior Upland is rich in natural resources. Minnesota's iron ore lies in this region. Some of the area's forests are in the Boundary Waters Canoe Area and in Voyageurs National Park.

Young Drift Plains

About 12,000 years ago, the last of the region's four glaciers covered most of Minnesota. These slow-moving sheets of ice scraped and smoothed the land's surface. They made lake basins. As glaciers melted, water filled the basins and created lakes. The glaciers left rich soil called drift and rolling hills called moraines.

The Young Drift Plains includes the Red River Valley, one of the nation's flattest areas. Melting glaciers created Lake Agassiz. The lake once covered parts of Canada, Iowa, and Minnesota. When the lake drained, rich soil and marshes remained.

Southern Regions

Rich till soil covers the Dissected Till Plains in southwestern Minnesota. The soil is a mix of sand, gravel, and clay. The soil and the warmer climate make the area good for crops and livestock. Most of the region's farmers often plant corn and soybeans.

Glaciers did not touch the Driftless Area in southeastern Minnesota. The rest of the state probably looked like this hilly region before the time of the glaciers. The Mississippi River flows

Minnesota's Land Features

through the area, forming the state's southeastern border. Apple orchards are common along the Mississippi River Valley.

Lakes and Rivers

Although Minnesota's license plates say "Land of 10,000 Lakes," there are actually more than 11,000 lakes in the state. Depending on how lake is defined, there are as many as 15,000. Lake resorts are a big part of Minnesota's tourism. Lake Itasca in the central part of the state is where the Mississippi River begins.

Minnesota's rivers flow out of the state into three different bodies of water. The Mississippi River drains to the south, all the

The headwaters of the Mississippi River mark the spot at Lake Itasca where the river begins.

Did you know...?
Mud Lake is the name of 201 Minnesota lakes. Long Lake is the name of 154 lakes, and Rice Lake is the name of 123. Only one lake is named Mugwump Lake.

way to the Gulf of Mexico. The Red River of the North flows north to Hudson Bay. The St. Louis River flows south into Lake Superior.

Climate

Cold winters and hot, humid summers are part of life in Minnesota. Heavy snowfall and blizzards are usual in winter. Thunderstorms are common in summer.

The coldest weather strikes northern Minnesota. In January, northern Minnesota temperatures average 15 degrees Fahrenheit (8 degrees Celsius) colder than the temperatures in southern Minnesota. In July, temperatures differ by only 5 degrees Fahrenheit (3 degrees Celsius).

Wildlife

Minnesota's lakes are home to many types of birds and fish. Bald eagles and great blue herons live near Minnesota lakes. People fish in the lakes for walleye, northern pike, muskie, and bass.

Loons, the Minnesota state bird, are common near many northern lakes. They dive to catch fish, frogs, and leeches. Their warning cry sounds like laughter. Loons call out to their lost family members with a wail. The sound is much like a wolf's howl.

Minnesota's land supports many types of mammals. Timberwolves roam through the northern forests. Moose, black bear, and white-tailed deer also are common. Beavers, muskrats, and river otters make their homes near water. The striped gophers dig holes across the prairie. The little animals gave Minnesota one of its nicknames, the Gopher State.

Environmental Threat

Pollution became a threat in the 1960s. A taconite mine dumped dangerous waste products into Lake Superior. In 1980, the state legislature ordered the mines to clean the lake. Mines had to find another dumping site.

In recent years, animal feedlots have caused problems. Feedlot manure decays and can create hydrogen sulfide, which smells like rotten eggs. This gas can be harmful to people. The Minnesota Pollution Control Agency now controls the location and type of feedlots.

Named the state bird in 1961, loons are often seen nesting on northern Minnesota lakes. Both male and female loons raise the young, which usually hatch in June. In August, loons prepare to migrate to the East Coast or to the Gulf of Mexico.

Dakota Indians lived in the Minnesota area when European explorers first arrived.

Chapter 3

History of Minnesota

In the 1600s, the Dakota and Ojibwa Indians lived in what is now Minnesota. The Ojibwa lived near the Great Lakes. The Dakota lived in the forests of northern Minnesota. Both tribes harvested wild rice, berries, and maple syrup. They also hunted and fished.

French and British Exploration

The first European explorers to come to the area were from France. In 1659 and 1660, two men explored the Great Lakes region, including northeastern Minnesota. They were Pierre Esprit Radisson and Medard Chouart, known as Sieur des Groseilliers. They wanted to find a water route across North America.

In 1679, Daniel Greysolon, known as Sieur Duluth, met with the Dakota Indians by Mille Lacs Lake. He claimed the area. Duluth traded furs and became friends with the Dakota.

Several other French fur traders explored the area in the late 1600s. They hoped to make money for France.

In 1763, France lost its North American lands to Great Britain. The British continued the search for a water route to the Pacific Ocean.

United States Gains Control

After the Revolutionary War (1775–1783), the United States received eastern Minnesota from Great Britain. Western Minnesota was part of the 1803 Louisiana Purchase.

In the early 1800s, the British tried to control U.S. shipping trade. They also forced Americans into service. The actions were among the reasons for the War of 1812 (1812–1814). During the war, the United States fought the British over the Great Lakes area. The Dakota and Ojibwa fought on Great Britain's side. The Indians were afraid Americans would form colonies in the area if they won the war. The Treaty of Ghent ended the war and allowed the United States to keep the land.

American Indians and settlers often visited Fort Snelling. The fort was located where the Minnesota and Mississippi Rivers met.

Surveying the Land

After the War of 1812, several military groups surveyed the land. Stephen H. Long wanted a military post where the Minnesota and Mississippi Rivers met. In 1820, Colonel Josiah Snelling's troops began building a fort. They wanted a place to defend against attacks from any direction. It was first named St. Anthony after the nearby waterfalls. In 1825, it was renamed Fort Snelling.

Fort Snelling was a busy gathering spot. The fort's location on two rivers brought many visitors to the steamboat port. It served as the first Indian Agency headquarters.

Wisconsin Territory

In 1836, the Wisconsin Territory was organized. It included eastern Minnesota. Western Minnesota was part of the Iowa Territory. The following year, the governor of Wisconsin

Territory urged Dakota and Ojibwa leaders to sign treaties. The Indians gave up their lands east of the Mississippi River.

Over the next 10 years, settlers started Minnesota's first towns. St. Paul, later the capital, was formed on the banks of the Mississippi River. The Falls of St. Anthony gave a source of power for the town of St. Anthony. People settled in the St. Croix River Valley, where Stillwater became a logging center.

When Wisconsin became a state in 1848, settlers in eastern Minnesota were left on their own. The area no longer had a territorial government or legal system.

The town of St. Anthony got its name from the nearby Falls of St. Anthony. Much of the historic village is now part of Minneapolis.

Treaty Trickery

Governor Alexander Ramsey (pictured) and Luke Lea met with Dakota chiefs at Traverse des Sioux in 1851. The chiefs signed a treaty. The chiefs thought the Dakota would receive full payment for selling their lands. The treaty specified payments over a 50-year period. Instead, some money that was meant to stay in tribal funds ended up going to pay debts to traders.

Minnesota Territory

Minnesota Territory was formed in 1849. Less than 4,000 settlers lived in eastern Minnesota. Settlers then wanted to add lands west of the Mississippi River.

Governor Alexander Ramsey and the Commissioner of Indian Affairs, Luke Lea, met with the Dakota in 1851. Treaties at Traverse des Sioux and Mendota resulted in more territory land.

During the mid-1800s, Minnesotans made land treaties with the Ojibwa. The Ojibwa sold forest areas from Lake Superior to the Red River. Indians sometimes received only a few cents an acre.

Joining the Union

By 1857, Minnesota's population had grown to more than 150,000 people. Henry Rice, Minnesota's delegate to Congress, suggested a bill for Minnesota's statehood.

Northerners favored the bill because it would add two more senators from nonslave states. Southerners did not want two new senators to change the Senate balance. After a few months of talk in Congress, Minnesota became the 32nd state on May 11, 1858.

> *Did you know...?*
> Minnesota did not have enough people to form a territory in 1849. The law required 5,000 people. U.S. Senator Stephen Douglas from Illinois claimed more than 8,000 people lived in Minnesota. A census taken after the territory had been formed showed a population of about 4,500.

Wars

During 1860 and 1861, 11 Southern states seceded from the United States. This action led to the Civil War (1861–1865). The Union and Confederacy fought over states' rights and slavery issues. Minnesota was the first state to offer troops to the North. More than 24,000 Minnesotans fought for the Union in the Civil War.

In the 1863 Battle of Gettysburg, the 1st Minnesota Regiment led an attack on the South's forces. The 1st

Minnesota Regiment lost 215 of its 262 members. The survivors helped win the battle the next day. They captured the flag of the 28th Virginia Regiment.

During the Civil War, Minnesota settlers and the Dakota disagreed over land issues. The Dakota thought the treaties were unfair. In 1858, the government forced the Dakota to sell part of their reservation land. The Dakota waited for payments promised to them by the U.S. government.

During the Civil War, members of the 4th Minnesota Infantry were among the 24,000 Minnesotans who fought for the Union.

"The 1st Minnesota rushed through the storm of bullets . . . with nothing but death to look for. . . . And, not a man wavered."

—Lieutenant William Lochren, describing the 1st Minnesota at the Civil War's Battle of Gettysburg

No payment came. In 1862, the Dakota were angry and hungry. The Dakota Conflict began when some Indians took control of the Lower Sioux Agency.

The Dakota, led by Chief Little Crow, attacked farms and killed settlers. Henry Sibley led troops to protect the settlers. Sibley's troops defeated the Dakota at the last battle near Wood Lake. Chief Little Crow left Minnesota along with other Dakota.

Sibley met with the Dakota who stayed behind. He tried to find out which of the men joined in the attacks on settlers. He named a five-man military court to try the Indians. The court ruled that 321 men were guilty. Most of these Indians were sentenced to death.

Bishop Henry Whipple disagreed with the punishment. He asked President Abraham Lincoln to pardon the men. Lincoln ordered jail terms for most of the Dakota. On December 26, 1862, the other 38 Dakota men were hanged in Mankato.

In the late 1800s, Minneapolis was known as the "Mill City." C. C. Washburn built his first flour mill near St. Anthony Falls. The milling company eventually became known as General Mills.

More Population Growth

The Homestead Act of 1862 gave each settler 160 acres (65 hectares) of free land. Settlers promised to build a house and live on the land for five years. By 1880, more than 62,000 land claims had been made in Minnesota.

". . . In the past 150 years, immigrants from more than 60 countries came to Minnesota, creating a state which may seem homogeneous but enjoys a legacy of rich cultural diversity."

—Dan Gunderson, reporter, in a 1999 Minnesota Public Radio story

Railroad companies, settlers, and others called for people to come to the area. Many Germans arrived in the 1850s. They settled in the town of New Ulm and in Stearns County.

Scandinavian immigrants began settling in the area in the 1800s. From 1870 to 1900, many Scandinavian immigrants came to the state. They often wrote letters home that described America as a wonderful place. The promise of a better life brought more immigrants from overseas and from other parts of the country.

Early Industries

Many immigrants turned to farming. By 1860, wheat became the leading crop. Wheat planted in the spring was harvested in late summer. Farmers also grew corn, potatoes, and oats.

During the 1860s, flour milling became one of the state's top industries. Mills started in the state's southern areas, including plants that opened in Minneapolis. For 50 years, the city was known as the "Mill City." Plants that opened there later became known as Pillsbury and General Mills.

Did you know...?

In 1914, the Red River Lumber Company printed a booklet with cartoons of Paul Bunyan. As Paul became well known, the stories grew more amazing. Paul was a giant with a big blue ox named Babe. Stories said that he dug out Lake Superior with his shovel, and that the many lakes in Minnesota were made from Babe's footprints.

In 1870, Edmund La Croix, a Minnesota inventor, invented a machine to produce finer, whiter flour. Demand for spring wheat flour increased.

Logging became an important industry in Minnesota's early years. Large white pine trees were easy to split into strong, straight boards.

The fastest way to transport lumber was to float the logs on rivers. The St. Croix River Valley became a large logging center. Winona was also a lumbering trade center. Lumber and logs were major state exports. The logging industry peaked in 1899.

In 1884, iron ore was first mined on the Vermilion Range in northern Minnesota. A few years later, iron ore was discovered on the Mesabi range. Hibbing, Virginia, Tower, and other towns became mining centers in northern Minnesota. By 1900, Minnesota was the leading U.S. producer of iron.

Great Depression

The Great Depression (1929–1939) affected Minnesota farmers and business leaders. Crop and livestock prices fell. Businesses could no longer count on sales from only one product for income.

Both farmers and businesses survived the depression by trying new things. Some farmers began raising soybeans. Businesses invented new products to increase markets.

Lumbermen in Minnesota found that the best way to move logs was to transport them on rivers. The log drivers were also called "river pigs."

In the early 1900s, Minnesota led the nation in iron ore production. These miners worked on the Mesabi Iron Range in Eveleth.

Mid-1900s

World War II (1939–1945) helped state and national economies recover after the Great Depression. Minnesota supplied food for soldiers and iron for equipment.

Minnesotans saw growth and change after the war. Manufacturing brought more money than did agriculture.

Iron mining had a record year in 1951. But soon the mines used most of the high-quality iron ore. In 1956, the first taconite mine opened in Silver Bay. This lower-grade ore was produced in pellets. The ore was shipped to steel mills in the East.

People in Canada and the United States thought business could increase if the Great Lakes connected to the Atlantic Ocean. In 1959, the St. Lawrence Seaway opened. It directly connected the Atlantic Ocean to Duluth. This northeastern city became the nation's most inland port.

In 1968, about 200 American Indians formed the American Indian Movement (AIM) in Minneapolis. The group led several national protests. These protests included the Trail of Broken Treaties in 1972 and the Longest Walk to Washington in 1978.

Late 1900s

In the 1980s, a slowdown in the economy affected farmers and ironworkers. Demand for iron ore decreased. Many workers lost jobs. For farmers, the 1988 drought resulted in crop loss and more debt.

The state of Minnesota values education. In 1987, Minnesota became the first state to allow school choice. School choice allows elementary and secondary school students to attend schools outside their neighborhoods or hometowns.

In 1992, the nation's largest indoor shopping center opened in Bloomington. The Mall of America offers an indoor amusement park called Camp Snoopy, an underwater park, and many specialty stores.

Minnesota's state capitol in St. Paul is the state's third capitol building.

Chapter 4

Government and Politics

Minnesotans are active in government. Minnesota usually has high voter turnout. In the 2002 state election, more than 60 percent of Minnesota voters cast ballots. It was the highest turnout in the country. Same-day voter registration allows voters to register at the polling place.

Minnesota's Government

In the 1850s, people had to agree on a constitution before gaining statehood. In 1857, the Democrats and Republicans held separate conventions. Each party had its own ideas. A committee of five men settled differences and wrote the state constitution.

Minnesota's government works much like the federal government. The three branches are called the executive, legislative, and judicial. These branches provide checks and balances. The system keeps one group from becoming stronger than the others.

The governor leads Minnesota's executive branch. This branch has more than 20 departments. These agencies carry out laws and policies in the state.

The state legislature includes the house and the senate. The legislature meets every other year, unless the governor calls a special session. Lawmakers make laws for the state. These laws usually deal with the state's taxes, programs, and policies.

Minnesota's judicial system has three levels. They are the district courts, court of appeals, and state supreme court.

Partisan Politics

Democrat Henry Sibley served as Minnesota's first governor from 1858 to 1860. After Sibley left the governor's office, Republicans held the office until 1898.

Minnesota's Government

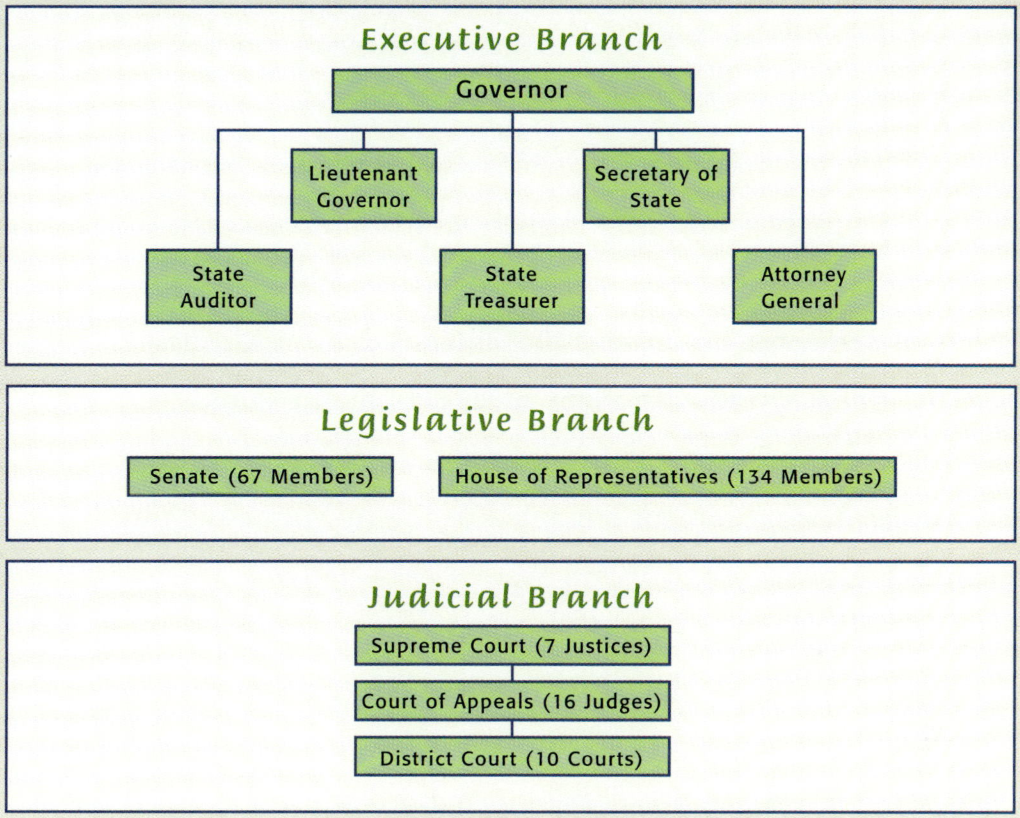

Minnesota citizens often use their government and politics to cause change. Minnesota has a history of creating and voting for third parties.

Hard times in the 1890s led farmers to form the Populist Party. Members believed in more rules for businesses,

". . . You don't have to be a career politician to serve in public office. You don't have to be well-connected or propped up by special-interest groups. You don't even have to be Democrat or Republican."
—Former Minnesota Governor Jesse Ventura

especially for railroads. The party also believed increasing the money supply would help farmers and laborers. Several Populists were elected to the state legislature in the 1890s.

In 1899, the Progressive movement began in Minnesota. This group agreed with many ideas held by the Populists. Progressives also worked for economic, social, and political change. The movement remained strong in Minnesota until attention switched to World War I (1914–1918).

In the 1920s and 1930s, the Farmer-Labor Party gained power. It stood for the interests of farmers, factory workers, and miners. In 1944, the Farmer-Labor Party joined with the Democrats. They became the Democratic Farmer-Labor (DFL) Party. The DFL remains a strong political force in the state.

Governor Floyd Olson was elected three times on the Farmer-Labor ticket. He was elected in 1930, 1932, and 1934. Olson saw the state through much of the Great Depression. He created unemployment programs. The state income tax was passed in 1933, during his second term.

In 1938, the Republicans returned to power. Republican Harold Stassen was elected governor. Republicans held many state offices until DFLer Hubert H. Humphrey was elected

No Alcohol Allowed

Minnesota Congressman Andrew J. Volstead supported outlawing the sale of alcohol. In 1919, the 18th Amendment was passed. It outlawed the sale of alcohol. Volstead supported the amendment. He also wrote the Volstead Act. This act gave authorities the power to enforce the amendment. Volstead is also known as the "father of prohibition." Prohibition lasted for 13 years.

senator in 1948. He served until 1964 and came back to office in 1971. He then served until his death in 1978.

National Recognition

Respected as a senator, Humphrey became a national figure as a U.S. vice president. From 1965 to 1968, he served as vice president under President Lyndon B. Johnson. In 1968, Humphrey was the Democratic candidate for president. He lost to Richard M. Nixon.

Minnesota's Walter F. Mondale also served as a U.S. vice president. Mondale, a Democrat, was elected in 1976 with Jimmy Carter. The two were defeated by Ronald Reagan and

and George Bush in the 1980 election. Mondale ran for president in 1984, but President Reagan was re-elected.

In 1969, President Nixon appointed two Minnesotans to the U.S. Supreme Court. Warren E. Burger was named the court's chief justice. President Nixon also named Minnesotan Harry Blackmun to the court.

Modern Issues

Minnesota's taxes are higher than those of many other midwestern states. In 1961, employers began taking state income tax from every employee's paycheck. A sales tax passed in 1967. Property taxes have always been high in Minnesota.

In recent times, a division has grown between the Twin Cities and other areas of the state. Increased population has given political power to the Twin Cities metro area of Minneapolis, St. Paul, and surrounding communities. Other Minnesota citizens sometimes hesitate to pay taxes for programs that only help the Twin Cities.

In the late 1990s, Minnesota and other states won lawsuits against tobacco companies. The lawsuits said companies knew their products were harmful. They also claimed cigarette advertising targeted teenagers.

In 2000, state funding from the tobacco settlement helped Minnesota teens form Target Market. This group uses TV and radio ads to educate the state's teenagers about smoking. Target Market points out the habit-forming and harmful things found in cigarettes. They also focus on health problems caused by smoking. By 2002, the group numbered 32,000 members.

Minnesota surprised the nation in 1998 by electing Jesse Ventura as governor. Ventura was once a professional wrestler. He was a third party candidate, running under the Reform Party. In 2000, Ventura and others broke away from the national Reform Party and created the Independence Party.

Hubert H. Humphrey served Minnesotans as a U.S. Senator for more than 20 years. During the 1960s, he also served as vice president for President Lyndon B. Johnson.

Throughout Minnesota, agriculture remains a strong economic force. Many families have farmed for several generations.

Chapter 5

Economy and Resources

Wheat was Minnesota's leading crop in the late 1800s. But in the 1900s demand for wheat declined. By the Great Depression of the 1930s, farmers and business people had begun to change their focus. Farmers began diversifying by growing different crops. Businesses like General Mills began making breakfast cereals and ready-made bread.

Researchers found a type of corn suited for Minnesota's short growing season. Corn and vegetable production also led to new food companies. In 1903, the Minnesota Valley Canning Company began in Le Sueur. The company later became known as Green Giant.

3M Inventions

3M researcher Art Fry developed the first use for Post-it Notes. He found a use for an adhesive invented by Dr. Spencer Silver, his co-worker. Silver's invention stuck to surfaces but left no sticky mess when removed. In the early 1970s, Fry was in search of a bookmark that wouldn't fall out of his church songbook. He solved his problem by using some of Silver's invention. Fry is shown here with other 3M products.

In the mid-1900s, soybeans became a popular crop. Soybean oil is used in shortening, margarine, and salad oil.

Minnesota farmers also raise livestock. Southern Minnesota dairy farmers found markets for milk, butter, and other products. Corn-rich southern Minnesota became a center for raising hogs. As a result, meatpacking companies started. In 1891, Hormel, best known as the maker of SPAM, began in Austin.

Minnesota and North Dakota lead the nation in sugar beet production. Most sugar beets are grown in the Red River Valley.

Technology Industry

Minnesota's best-known and largest high-tech company is 3M, headquartered in St. Paul. In 1902, it began as Minnesota Mining and Manufacturing in Two Harbors. Its first product was sandpaper. The 3M company has created many products, including self-stick tape, Post-it Notes, and Scotchgard.

Computer industries employ many Minnesotans. Hardware and software companies, such as IBM in Rochester, are manufacturing centers for computers.

Service Industries

Service industries represent the largest part of Minnesota's economy. Hotels and travel agencies, health services, childcare services, and libraries are all examples of service industries.

Many of Minnesota's service industries are known outside of the state. The Mayo Clinic located in Rochester offers world-famous medical care. The Mayo Clinic is a worldwide leader in research about cancer and other diseases. Offices are also located in Florida and Arizona.

Tourists help boost the state's economy. Twin Cities attractions and sporting events bring tourists to the state. In addition, visitors come to Minnesota lakes to swim, waterski, sailboat, fish, and hunt. Northwest Airlines, headquartered in the Twin Cities area, flies visitors to the state. In 2000, tourism brought $9 billion into the state and supported 129,700 jobs. The industry grew 31 percent from 1996 to 2000.

Iron Ore

The Mesabi Iron Range of northeastern Minnesota saw success in the 1950s. When mining used up most of the high-quality iron ore, researchers found a way to process a

lower-grade ore. The ore, called taconite, was more expensive to produce than high-grade iron ore.

In 1963, a law stopped any increase in taconite taxes for 25 years. As a result, production increased and more taconite plants were built. The plants developed new machines that worked directly with the ore. The workers maintain and repair the machines. Although a 2001 plant closing in Hoyt Lakes laid off nearly 1,200 workers, taconite mining continues to be an important part of Minnesota industry.

The Mississippi River flows near the hub of the downtown Minneapolis area.

The Oldenberg Sculpture rests in the sculpture garde
outside the Walker Art Center in Minneapolis.

Chapter 6

People and Culture

Although once mostly an agricultural state, Minnesota has changed its focus since 1940. More than twice as many Minnesotans live in cities as live in rural areas. Urban growth has led to more cultural events for Minnesota residents and visitors. Theater, dance, and art galleries are popular.

Minnesota's Ethnic Backgrounds

White people are the largest population group in Minnesota. African Americans form the second largest ethnic group. Many African Americans have come to the

Did you know...?
The first enclosed shopping mall in the United States was built in Edina, Minnesota, in 1956. The Southdale Shopping Mall still serves customers today.

state since the 1940s. Asians began moving into the state in the late 1900s. Hmong came in the 1980s from Laos, Vietnam, and Thailand. In the late 1990s and early 2000s, Somalis escaped their war-torn country in Africa and moved to Minnesota.

Minnesota Arts

Minnesotans support the arts. The Guthrie Theater, located in Minneapolis, is a national leader in theater. Each year, more than 340,000 people attend the Minneapolis Children's Theatre. The company presents performances for the public and for schools.

Art centers are favorite cultural choices. The Walker Art Center in Minneapolis displays visual art. The center also has programs for dancers and other performing artists. The Minneapolis Institute for the Arts includes exhibits that span 5,000 years of history. It is recognized as one of the best museums in the nation.

Minnesotans also focus on music. The St. Paul Chamber Orchestra and the Minnesota Orchestra perform classical and

Minnesota's Ethnic Backgrounds

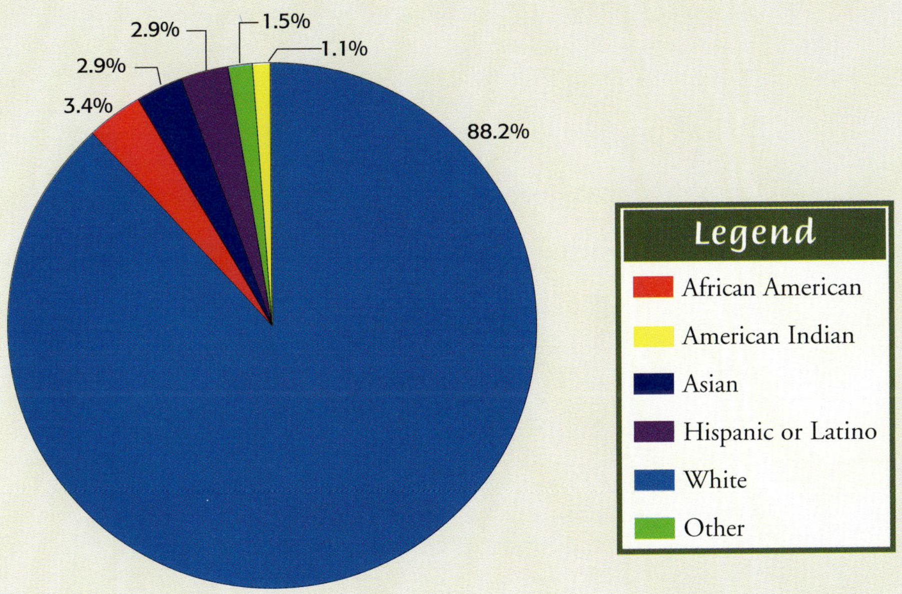

modern music. Colleges and universities such as Minnesota State University Moorhead, Gustavus Adolphus, Concordia College in Moorhead, and St. Olaf have nationally recognized music programs. Duluth, a center for jazz music, features the Bayfront Blues Festival each August.

Minnesota Writers

Several famous writers came from Minnesota. F. Scott Fitzgerald of St. Paul became well known in the 1920s. He wrote *The Great Gatsby* and other novels about society. Sinclair Lewis was born in Sauk Centre. He wrote 62 novels, including *Main Street,* which is set in small-town Minnesota. Lewis received the 1930 Nobel Prize for Literature. Garrison Keillor is both an author and a radio personality known for his National Public Radio show, *A Prairie Home Companion.*

Charles M. Schulz, born in Minneapolis, was a writer and cartoonist. Schulz, who died in 2000, was most famous for his comic strip *Peanuts.* The comic strip began in 1950. TV specials featuring *Peanuts* characters began in 1965 and still air today.

In 1996, Charles M. Schulz, creator of the *Peanuts* comic strip, received a star on Hollywood's Walk of Fame. Sculptures of Schulz' characters have been created throughout the Twin Cities area.

"People think they can make a difference here. If my nose freezes shut, it's a beautiful price to pay for a great way of life."

—Kate DiCamillo, children's book author, after moving back to Minnesota from Florida

Several writers of children's books have also come from Minnesota. Some of Laura Ingalls Wilder's *Little House* books told of pioneer life in Minnesota. Minnesota author Kate DiCamillo received a 2001 Newbery Honor Medal for her novel, *Because of Winn-Dixie*. Minnesota author Gary Paulsen writes wilderness and adventure stories. He has written more than 80 books.

Sports

Minnesota is home to several professional sports teams, including the Vikings football team and the Twins baseball team. Other professional teams with a Minnesota home base include the Wild hockey team and the Chill volleyball team. Minnesota is home to two professional basketball teams. The NBA Timberwolves and the WNBA Lynx are based in the Twin Cities.

Recreation for All Weather

Minnesota is known for being cold. But Minnesotans pride themselves on being tough enough to withstand the winters. Many residents enjoy cross-country skiing and snowmobiling. Two snowmobiling companies are headquartered in Minnesota. Polaris is in Roseau, and Arctic Cat is in Thief River Falls.

Minnesota summers are hot and humid. Minnesotans cool off by traveling to the lakes. Some people have lake cabins where they stay on weekends and during vacations.

Did you know...?
The sport of waterskiing was invented in Minnesota. Ralph Samuelson built the first pair of water-skis in 1922. He rode them behind a boat on Lake Pepin.

The Future

The past, present, and future are joined together in Minnesota. Visitors and residents enjoy the wide range of activities and events. The state continues to offer a rich cultural heritage. Agriculture remains strong. Continued growth, expansion, and development give the state new hopes for the future.

Minnesota Twins third baseman Corey Koskie slides into base. Koskie played for the Twins during the 2002 season when the team qualified for the playoffs.

Recipe: Blueberry Muffins

Blueberries grow wild in the northeastern forests of the state. The blueberry muffin is the official state muffin.

Ingredients

½ cup (120 mL) butter, softened
1¼ cups (300 mL) sugar
2 eggs
2 cups (480 mL) flour
½ teaspoon (2.5 mL) salt
2 teaspoons (10 mL) baking powder
½ cup (120 mL) milk
2 cups (480 mL) blueberries
3 teaspoons (15 mL) sugar
1 teaspoon (5 mL) orange peel, grated

Equipment

dry-ingredient measuring cups
liquid measuring cups
measuring spoons
electric hand mixer
large mixing bowl
2 small mixing bowls
fork
muffin pan
muffin cup liners or nonstick cooking spray

1. Preheat oven to 375°F (190°C).
2. Use a hand mixer to mix the butter and 1 ¼ cups sugar in a large bowl. Mix until light and creamy. Add eggs one at a time, beating well after each.
3. Mix the flour, salt, and baking powder together in a small bowl.
4. Add a little of the dry mixture to the egg and butter mixture. Then add a little of the milk. Alternate the dry mixture and milk until used.
5. Crush ½ cup blueberries with a fork in a small bowl. Mix into batter. Mix in the remaining whole berries and add orange peel.
6. Put muffin cup liners into the muffin pan cups or spray muffin pan cups with nonstick cooking spray.
7. Fill cups about ⅔ full.
8. Sprinkle tops with 3 teaspoons sugar. Bake for 20 to 30 minutes. Remove from oven. Cool for 30 minutes before removing from muffin pan.

Makes 6 servings

Minnesota's Flag and Seal

Minnesota's Flag

The state seal appears in the middle of Minnesota's royal blue flag. The flag is fringed in gold. A wreath of lady's slippers refers to the state flower. The 19 stars around the wreath represent the states that joined the Union after the original 13 colonies. The largest star stands for Minnesota, which was the 19th state to join the Union after the original 13.

Minnesota's State Seal

Used on official papers and documents, the Minnesota seal stands for the state's government. A scene of Minnesota in its founding year shows a farmer plowing a field, the falls of St. Anthony, and an American Indian on horseback. Minnesota's motto is "The Star of the North." These words appear in French on the state seal.

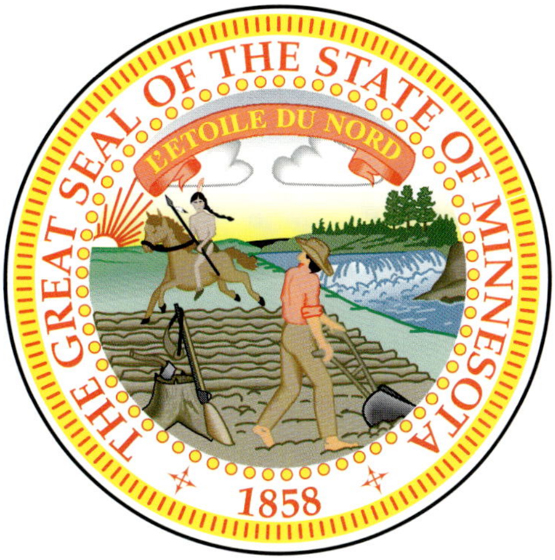

Almanac

General Facts

Nickname:
North Star State

Population: 4,919,479 (U.S. Census 2000)
Population rank: 21st

Capital: St. Paul

Largest cities:
Minneapolis, St. Paul, Duluth, Rochester, Bloomington

Geography

Area: 84,068 square miles (217,736 square kilometers)
Size rank: 12th

Highest point: Eagle Mountain, 2,301 feet (701 meters) above sea level

Lowest point: Along Lake Superior, 602 feet (183 meters) above sea level

Agriculture

Agricultural products:
Dairy, wheat, corn, soybeans, wild rice, hogs, beef cattle, sugar beets

Climate

Average summer temperature:
67 degrees Fahrenheit (19 degrees Celsius)

Average winter temperature:
12 degrees Fahrenheit (minus 11 degrees Celsius)

Average annual precipitation: 26 inches (66 centimeters)

Pink and white lady's slippers

Common loon

Symbols

Animal: White-tailed deer

Bird: Common loon

Fish: Walleye

Flower: Pink and white lady's slipper

Economy

Natural resources: Lumber, taconite

Types of Industry: Computers, medical devices, processed foods

Symbols

Mineral: Lake Superior agate

Motto: Star of the North

Song: "Hail, Minnesota," Music and first verse by Truman E. Rickard, second verse by Arthur E. Upson

Tree: Norway pine

Government

First governor: Henry Sibley

Statehood: May 11, 1858 (32nd state)

U.S. Representatives: 8

U.S. Senators: 2

U.S. electoral votes: 10

Counties: 87

Timeline

State History

1600
Dakota and Ojibwa live in area that is now Minnesota.

1659–1660
Radisson and Groseillers, French explorers, are the first Europeans to come to Minnesota.

1783
United States receives part of Minnesota at the end of the Revolutionary War.

1820
Construction of Fort Snelling begins.

1863
Soldiers in the 1st Minnesota Regiment fight at the Battle of Gettysburg.

U.S. History

1620
Pilgrims establish a colony in the New World.

1775–1783
American colonists fight for their freedom in the Revolutionary War.

1812–1814
The United States and Great Britain fight the War of 1812.

1861–1865
The Union and Confederacy fight the Civil War.

1930s
Farmers and businesses diversify to survive the Great Depression.

1959
The St. Lawrence Seaway opens and creates a route from Duluth to the Atlantic Ocean.

1992
The largest U.S. mall, Mall of America, opens in Bloomington.

2000
Minnesota teens start Target Market, an anti-smoking campaign.

1914–1918
World War I is fought; the United States enters the war in 1917.

1929–1939
The United States experiences the Great Depression.

1939–1945
World War II is fought; the United States enters the war in 1941.

1964
U.S. Congress passes the Civil Rights Act, which makes discrimination illegal.

2001
On September 11, terrorists attack the World Trade Center and the Pentagon.

Words to Know

adhesive (ad-HEE-siv)—a substance, such as glue, that makes things stick together

alluvial (ah-LOO-vee-ahl)—made from soil carried and left by a river

diversify (di-VUR-suh-fye)—to increase the variety of something; many Minnesota businesses survived hard economic times by adding new items to their product lines.

glacier (GLAY-shur)—slow-moving sheet of ice

moraine (mu-RANE)—stone and earth deposits that form rolling hills

Populist Party (POP-yoo-list PAR-tee)—a political party in the late 1800s; the Populists believed in greater government regulation of business.

Progressive movement (PRO-gress-ive MOOV-muhnt)—a political movement that was strong in Minnesota in the early 1900s; Progressives shared many populist beliefs and called for economic, social, and political reforms.

taconite (TA-kuh-nite)—flint-like rock that forms a low-grade iron ore

To Learn More

Hintz, Martin. *Minnesota.* America the Beautiful. New York: Children's Press, 2000.

Porter, A. P. *Minnesota.* Hello U.S.A. Minneapolis: Lerner, 2002.

Schwabacher, Martin. *Minnesota.* Celebrate the States. Tarrytown, N.Y.: Benchmark Books, 1999.

Todd, Anne M. *The Ojibwa: People of the Great Lakes.* American Indian Nations. Mankato, Minn.: Bridgestone Books, 2003.

Internet Sites

Track down many sites about Minnesota.
Visit the FACT HOUND at *http://www.facthound.com*

IT IS EASY! IT IS FUN!

1) Go to *http://www.facthound.com*
2) Type in: 0736815910
3) Click on "FETCH IT" and FACT HOUND will find several links hand-picked by our editors.

FACT HOUND℠

Relax and let our pal FACT HOUND do the research for you!

Places to Write and Visit

Mall of America
Crossroads of Interstate 494 and Highway 77
60 East Broadway
Bloomington, MN 55425

Minnesota Children's Museum
10 West Seventh Street
St. Paul, MN 55102

Minnesota Historical Society
345 West Kellogg Boulevard
St. Paul, MN 55102-1906

Minnesota Office of Tourism
100 Metro Square
121 7th Place East
St. Paul, MN 55101-2146

The Mall of America, Bloomington, not only provides shopping, it also provides visitors with amusement park rides at Camp Snoopy located inside the mall.

Index